CROSSROADS

CROSSROADS

DRE HILL

atmosphere press

Thank you for meeting me where the roads cross.

✕ Dre Hill

this is for a boy that I once knew.
he was both brave and true.
I lost him in search of a man I'm still trying to find.
choosing to leave what I know behind.
forgive me gentlemen, both of you.

TABLE OF CONTENTS

the artist's prayer

humbly, I come asking these things

and many more

may my paint run freely

as I glide across the canvas

may the words I write

ignite a spark inside the heart

may my work be perceived

as I, the creator, intended

may my pieces travel the world

like missions of outreach

may many minds be changed

and artists raised as a result

may my work support my lifestyle

that I may spend my days creating

humbly, I ask these things

and more

amen

IN INNOCENCE

Childhood's Light

In the night of childhood

Under adulthood's moon

Burns the shadows that cause us fright

Let the sun of new life

Vanquish all things evil within our sight

And

Spark the fire of childhood's light

Mr. Stick [Wishbone]

my first real friend was Mr. Stick

it was an imaginary friend

with a very real body

one that I could never lose

he was shaped like a wishbone

clearly he was lucky—or magical—

I was convinced he had to be

he carried me from realm to realm

all the while acting as a guide

his face forever a friendly pudgy smile

penciled in with permanent marker

his eyes forever unblinking

stamped into his face like tiny black holes

the same kind we would summon

to travel between worlds

until mom called out dinner time

and he had to release me to her care

while he napped in the comfort of my room

A Pillow Named Scooby Doo

my first dog was a pillow
a pillow named Scooby-Doo
his fur was nonexistent
his features were all flat
my head laid on top of him
it often felt like I shattered his back
yet every day there he would lay
at the head of my bed
where I would snuggle my covers
and sleep like the dead
his cushion brought me comfort
with his tail coiled on my chest
his shriek brings me serenity
as at last, I get my rest

Sprinklers

When the sun sits up high
And the temperatures rise
Dad pulls out the
Sprinklers
We dance around the yard
In a tribal routine
Celebrating the reign of the water
And the coming of summer

Dysfunction

Sometimes my family is dysfunction
My siblings are chaos
My parents are anxiety
My cousins are drama and mess
Sometimes my family is dysfunction
It feels like antics in a circus
Or a restaurant with poor service
Or a beaten, bloody cervix
Sometimes my family is dysfunction
With their back-door dealings
And their jaded feelings
And bonds in need of healing
Sometimes my family is dysfunction
But they're still my family

Summer

On summer nights
I sleep semi nude
Mom doesn't cook much
So we make our own food

On summer days
I run in the morning
While it's still cool
Before you're cooked without warning

On summer nights
I dream of the beach
Playing in the sand
And swimming like a leech

On summer days
I stand under the hose
Trying to stay cool
Like a wilting brown rose

Gifted and Talented

I was identified as gifted and talented
it was the talk of the third-grade table
the way they ogled over me
surely that meant that I was special
that I was some child genius
a child prodigy with untapped potential
I thought I would be as magical as Harry Potter
or as extraordinary as the various X-Men
I knew it was fantasy, but a kid can dream
still, I expected something—anything
what I didn't expect was to go my whole childhood
not knowing what it truly meant

Death of the Kid

bow your head
let us mourn
shed your tears
whisper your prayers

the kid is dead

cherish his memory
taste his charisma
revel in his purity
ponder what could have been

the kid is dead

and you killed him

Deep End | One Peed

One

Two

Three

I hold my breath

I wait silently

The surface is still

A clean, crisp edge

One

Two

Three

I sit in the deep end

Letting my mind wander

Watching my thoughts expand

I am the calm pool

One

Two

Three

I am the deep end

Absorbing the sun

Prolonging my days

Changing the seasons

One

Two

Three

IN LOVE/LUST

Love

Love
I don't have it
What is it?
I've never known

Love, love
It comes from within
That's what they say
Some intrinsic feeling

It starts with yourself
From there it grows
You give it
Then it goes
As long as we've got

Love

Damn You're Such A-

When people ask me about you
I struggle with what to say
I want to blurt out what's true
But worry what that might convey

Damn you're such a
Prickly pain in my ass
With a love for confrontation
And a body full of sass

Damn you're such a
Sweet smelling honeybun
With a heart full of gold
That makes my life more fun

Damn you're such a
Fucking little child
Shrugging off responsibility
Like you live in the wild

Damn you're such a
Needless cause of strife
You bug me to no end
But I'll love you for the rest of my life

I Don't Want You

I don't want you
Not for your sparkling eyes
Or brilliant smile
Or even your beautiful face

I don't want you
Not for your heart of gold
Or your love of people
Or even your infectious positivity

I don't want you
Not for your athleticism
Or artistry
Or even your intellectual prowess

I do want you
For all those things combined
The love, joy, and passion
And more

XXX

They say love is blind
They
Were
Wrong

Love is not blind
It
Sees
All
And chooses to accept

Lust chooses what to see
It consumes the mind
Destroys the heart
Sex is blind

70 minus 1

Unilateral
A cyclical chain
Intertwined yin and yang
Two fish swimming in unison

Shift position
Adjusting weight
Bountiful pleasure
A test of fate

On the top
Side by side
On the bottom
The circle of 69

We Know

I know about her
Though you think I don't
Her scent wafts through the house
Her presence invades my home

I know about him
Though you try to hide it
He has you swishing when you walk
He has you changing how you talk

We know
That this won't work
Like a deep running scar
Ripping this band-aid will hurt

Waterfall Out of Love

Waterfall out of love
anger from above
rocks and slides
lightning filled skies
lost hopes and fears
blood boiling tears
that's what cheating does
when we waterfall out of love

Heart Full of Thorns

this is a song to my lover

the one with the supple lips

the face that's easy to kiss

the hug that melts me like butter

this is a serenade for my lover

the one with the heart full of thorns

the words that bruised without marks

the sassy quips and snarky remarks

the hands that gently crumpled my heart

this is a tune for my lover

the one who keeps moving forward

the one that kept me looping

the one who has my broken heart swooning

because you planted the seeds

for this heart full of thorns

Fuck Cupid

Fuck Cupid
Shooting arrows in the dark
Just to break my heart

Sloppy Cupid
Leaving me scarred with his mark
Making my love life Salvador Dalí art

Damned Cupid
With your fucking magic love spark
From my life I feel love depart

Fuck Cupid

I Don't Run for Love

I don't run for love

Not anymore

Not when I could scour the earth

Or beat my high score

I don't run for love

Not when it didn't run for me

Not when I cried for it

Or begged for it on bent knee

I don't run for love

Not when it's not mine

Not when it hurts my feelings

Or wastes my time

I don't run for love

IN MIND

What I Know

they say knowledge can't be stolen

I'm not sure that's true

after all

what we thought we knew

was recycled propaganda

old ideas

scrubbed to look new

I'm no longer sure

of

what I know

Signs

pisces sun, leo moon, aries rising

yet

still, that tells me nothing

perhaps

perhaps I have the wrong signs

red light, yellow light, green light

those

they tell me what to do

yet

still, that tells me nothing

perhaps

perhaps I have the wrong signs

whispers, visions, spirit guides

and

still, that tells me nothing

I

still look for some signs

because

I clearly have the wrong ones

In the Darkness

Here are the quiet moments
the whispering thoughts
eating
at your wayward soul
devouring your being.
Here are the lingering queries
clouding
your sense of direction
in a darkening haze
suggesting all that you lack.
Here are the patches of darkness
the voids where light fails
blotting
out your hopes and joys
with a flood of viscous tears
congesting you with reality.

Charmed

you have such good energy
they're intoxicated
inundated with a chemical connection
or so they perceive
because perception is everything
so they see charisma
in place of my charms
they feel good vibes
as the incantations roll off my tongue
they entrench themselves in my presence
as if it were not divinely ordained
their steps are ordered
their thoughts are planted
their eyes are fooled by illusion
and they perceive it without hesitation
without bated breath or batted eye
this is my witchcraft
to know people
to have people know of me
and love me

Blood Red Petals

my body is a record
covered in tally marks
nicked, bruised, and scratched
by the damning claws of reality
each new slice is a stinging lash
to the soft butter of my skin
the pain is my oldest friend
he coaxes me as I ooze
bleeding my suffering
onto the beautiful
blood red petals
of the roses that
I give to my
family and
friends

Intrusion

my reflection contorts
a devilish smile on its face
whispering the ways I could end myself

I do not want this
my protests—killed
as aliens wriggle to my brain
invading my privacy

this is the song of intrusion
an ominous ode
staccato notes beating
into the base of my skull

this is the song of intrusion
stuck on replay in my head
as I catch my hands
before I swerve into a ditch

this is the song of intrusion
stuck on replay in my head
as I catch my hands
before I slit my wrist

this is the song of intrusion
stuck on replay in my head
that shoots for death
but still maims me with a miss

The Monster Under My Bed

my eyes are closed tight
what I can't see can't see me
my heart is pounding apace
there's nothing to hear but the beat
my blanket covers my body
this thin veil is my only protection
my breath is rapid and shallow
with each breath I suffocate—gasping
there is no reprieve from the monster's call
all I can do is quietly steel my nerves
while tentacle or toe traipses about
this bed is a silver platter and I the meal
for the years of concealed illness
centuries of generational trauma
inexplicable newfound stresses
wrapped in the skin of my imagination
sleep will descend upon me soon
until its sweet release I must endure
the whispers will eventually cease
and the monster beneath me will fade

I am Confusion

I am confusion
Not because I don't know
Where I'm going
Even though I don't

I am confusion
Not because math is hard despite
What anyone says
And it is

I am confusion
Not because I'm actually confused
Or even surprised
And disappointment is all I feel

I am confusion
Because we teach kids morality
When we are immoral
Even hypocritical

I am confusion
Because we preach equality
Where it's not practiced
And pretend it works

I am confusion
Because this world is a refracted mirror
Constantly warping reflections
And I don't know what anything is
Not anymore

Perseverance

I was tired of crying

from sinking like the Titanic

watching the best parts of me drown

I was tired of breaking

from a shifting foundation

allowing me to collapse like a demolished building

I was tired of enduring

an unending cycle of abuse and neglect

like the gifts of the Earth that run dry and burn

I was tired of screaming

from a mouth that was always being covered

where my voice faded into an imperceptible whisper

I was tired of existing

but the sweet release of *surrender*

failed to compel me

instead a new vibration resonated—continuance

Drugged

rest little one
it's the invisible whisper
you don't hear
but your body feels

rest little one
resistance feels futile
as your eyelids droop
and your body weakens
but yet, you persist

rest little one
the fight is hard
the battle is long
and yet you're doomed to fail

rest little one
you succumb to sleep
fatigue is one hell of a drug
dissolving in your body like a pill in a drink

Assurance

Swallowed by the past
Drowning in right now
Darkness closing fast
Spirit giving out
Mama said to pray
Think that's all she knows
Slowly lose my way
That's just how it goes
Eyes are growing dry
Time just slips away
Almost time to fly
Night turns into day
Showed me how to cope
Going with the flow
Livin' off new hope
Not quite time to go

Mended

I don't wanna die
Kinda wanna live
Got so much to give
Feels like it's obvious

I don't wanna lie
Time is passing by
Scream until I cry
Who's gonna save me?

I guess I could try
Fight with all my might
Dusk to morning light
Just so I can be free

I know what I want
Stepping over stones
Mending all my bones
Healing in my own safety

I am who I am
Both feet on the ground
Not tripping now
What I lost, I've found

IN MEMORY

Give Up the Ghost

I am air

A sensation of experiences

Chained to mounds of flesh

Caged in stress and disorder

I am life

The rush of wind through hair

A stomach full of butterflies

A body lost in free fall

I am image

A series of interior reflections

The conjecture of several wild guesses

The unfinished sketch from my parents

I am ghost

Loosened from body and mind

Ethereal projection of life

Lasting image lost in the light

Desolate

heavy are the feet

scaling both ridge and mountain

dejected is the heart

beating out of rhythm

weary are the eyes

looking for the illumination of a new horizon

Shadow Work

without a moment's hesitation

I stepped off the precipice

releasing myself from my monument of counterfeit grins

to plummet into the darkness below

this is my journey into the unknown

where the façade meets the shadows that cradle my inner child

Cobwebs

oh, what a tangled web we weave

sliding down sound strands

of joy, anxiety, and depression that

stitch and bind us together,

cascading in intricate ornamentations

of hair bows, wedding rings, and cracked bottles

that fasten tightly at the point

of our sticky intersections.

oh, what silky viscous threads of

sentiment connect us at

the nexus of our humanity

manifesting through interaction,

as we navigate a series of

identities and their attributes

intertwined in the fiber of others.

oh, what viscid gossamer rope

that tugs and pulls on the heart

as it swells with the passions of love and anger

or shatters with sadness and fear,

plaited in an intricate pattern of

crisscross designs that spell

out the stories of kindergarten crushes,

buried matriarchs, and new chapters.

Music

music has become my medication
see my daily meditation, it ain't working

smile on my face, of course I'm faking
all this ignorance and evil been gestating

my peace been shattered, my faith is quaking
all this hatred waiting, love overtaken

so the lyrics take me
beats bathe me
melody saves me

shed some tears
releasing fears

perhaps I'll sleep tonight.

416

There's a house on Calhoun

It's not hard to miss

The wooden stairs creak

The floorboards hiss

Walls like paper

Fragile and thin

They contain nothing

Secrets simply walk in

A quaint house indeed

With a basement to boot

A spacious cavern

Causing screams and hoots

There's a house on Calhoun

Its address is 416

I lived there once

Those days I sometimes miss

With the wooden stairs that hiss

And the late-night screams

Followed by early mornings with the team

There were days of stress

Followed by nights of no rest

Though pain was around

Love rained down

In that house on Calhoun

Unspoken

The silence is telling
nothing is said
And yet, the understanding
is unspoken
At least that's what I thought

If I could take us back
If I could just do that
Then I would rewrite the stars
mend your wounds and scars
And shatter the silence
to speak what's unspoken
And fix what's been broken

5:24

you don't fear death, right?
not as your life flashes before your eyes
rolling in across the horizon from your left
a silent crashing wave—it pummels into you
a phantasmic assailant

a phantasmic assailant
one that swims through molasses
seen in full before it is perceived
right until the point of impact
where I am overtaken

where I am overtaken
violently thrown into the brush
a body of motion—stalled in place
the tiniest field of flowers
like a final resting place

like a final resting place
surely a part of me has died
a sliver of my spirit unleashed
to watch over this hallowed ground
you don't fear death, right?

you don't fear death, right?
not as your heart beats out your chest
red and blue lights washing over you
held tight in the softest, warmest embrace
as you leave behind the husk of what was

the street on which my heart beats

follow the ever-winding path

it's a road called Trinity Blvd

skin slick with the tears of the sky

raining down to kiss the Earth in appreciation

here—Trinity Blvd—I see in my dreams

my heart claws out of my chest

tires slip into the grass and mud

mirrors are thrown to the wind

it's on a road called Trinity Blvd

where I lost my heart to asphalt

and gained trauma to take its place

Re: Memory

this is for those who ask

do you remember when?

oblivious

unawares of the intended

regression and suppression of that time

place

or person

for the sake of fortitude

and the sanctuary of sanity

I

will not

remember

Take Me Home

please
take me home
to the time before
I long for blissful
ignorance

please
take me home
to a faraway land
I miss my youthful
innocence

please
take me home
to a space that is not here
to a life that is not this
to a sanctuary
please

2420

It was not my first house
But it is my forever home
Where my childhood flourished
And my imagination roamed

Within its walls I grew
Under its roof I tried
Between the corners I hid
Atop the furniture I cried

I'm older now, time to fly
But I'll try to visit often
Wherever your heart is, your home is too
And that house makes my heart soften

IN IDENTITY

Gaunt

oh you're so skinny!
thank you
that's what one says, right?
as if I'm unaware of my form
or the actual object of envy

I want to be skinny like you!
thank you
that's what one says, right?
as if I chose this body
or desire to stay in it

thank you
that's what one says, right?
as if I like to receive it
or the words are compliments
not bricks shattering my confidence

· *that's what one says, right?*
as if I ever wanted any of this
or require your objectification
in a world where I take up little space
the lightness weighing on me constantly

This Skinny Body

I know it was a joke

lighthearted

good in nature

but it was the catalyst

the culling of my confidence

the cesser of my self-worth

I'm not like the other boys

my physique doesn't impose

I cannot crush with my palms

much less open tight jars

I struggle with lifting things

despite moving with the wind

I eye other bodies enviously

do I want to be them or their body?

to be seen and felt as a god

a living testament to divine inspiration

for now, I'll settle for the cheerios

as I bounce them against my hip

a ridiculous ritual of hula hoop

for one such as myself

as my ribs kiss the sun

and my bones press to break the skin

Asthma Pump

Hurf
this is the second wind
it tickles the throat
swims through the blood
and fills the lungs

Hurf
this is resuscitation
it is the kiss of life
a return of the soul
sucked clean from the body

Hurf
this is the breath of God
it endows with divinity
expelling death's vapors
with each puff of oxygen

Hemoglobin

the moment the needle enters my arm

where the metal rips a hole in me

and my vein puckers for a kiss

that is the moment I lose track of my senses

my body is no longer my own

instead it belongs to another

as my veins reject the needle

leaving me with clammy palms

while duplicates multiply into a haze

I slowly sink into the darkness

pulled back above the choppy waters

only by the bent plastic of an apple juice cup

and the reassuring voice echoing in my ear

as the needle once again slides inside my body

this is my most perfect purgatory

a molestation of my broken mind

the repeated abuse of my body

I watch, defenseless, as the needle plunges into me

injecting me with screaming euphoria

inciting an operatic crescendo of pain and nausea

that fades only when the bandages are on

and I am sent on my way at the end of my check up

HuMaN

this is the story of my life
a lament for my purity
but also a love letter
written in my own blood
bound in the sinew of my body

this is the erasure of my past
burnt to ash in the fires of religion
my future is bound on a spindle
stitching together a new Frankenstein
tethering demons in the caricature of my flesh

this is the assault of my mind
penetrated daily by doctrine
it is also the seduction of my heart
tongues lash cuts into the organ
bleeding my feelings onto the floor

this is the death of my identity
slaughtered by society's scripture
my reflection is shattered
creating a disillusioned mosaic
refracting the halo into horns

this is the birth of my anger
the labor of oppression

but also a soothing kiss

that quells the hatred within

while kindness is channeled like a spirit

Through the Wire

I took talking for granted
And then I couldn't anymore
There was blood
And gauze
And wires galore

I took walking for granted
And then I couldn't do it unaided
My body weakened
And everything hurt
And life's light faded

I took pain for granted
And then I felt it every single day
There was choking
And ribs poking
And existential suicidal decay

I took dry eyes for granted
And then I never stopped crying
Over grunts through the wire
And a body on fire
And a boy who felt like dying

Repudiation

rejection hurts

you present yourself—all of yourself

your scars

your flaws

your wounds still healing

bare, naked to the world

and say—here I am, judge me

again

and again

and again

the world will say you are not enough

you are not the best

you are not what I want

time and time again

you bear yourself bare

you bear yourself naked

and the world takes a little bit of you saying

no, not enough—not right, not what I want

but the other thing about rejection is this

the world is not who you write for

the world is not who you live for

the world is not who you submit for

you submit for yourself

you lay yourself bare—naked

with the hopes someone sees you

sees you

sees your experience—sees your journey

sees your trauma, scars, and flaws

and understands you in a fundamental way

because they themselves have lain naked before the world

and been rejected

Tipsy

In my cup is power
I drink from it every hour
Sometimes darkness abounds
When there is no light around
It tickles my throat
It warms my chest
Deep from within it draws me out
It causes some to yell and others to shout
One cup, two cup, three cups now
They marvel and ask me how
I thirst for more
I pour one up
There's a slight buzzing sound
As we all gather round
Singing songs into the night
Not a care in the world in sight
I might be a little tipsy

Twenty-Two

Life is what you make it
Or so I've been told
To be honest, I can't fake it
I'm not that bold

Once I was seven years old
Then I was seventeen
Now I'm twenty-two
But still lonely and don't know what to do

Life is what you make it
But I can't build shit
I don't like getting dirty
Unless I'm getting fit

Young, dumb, and clueless
Twenty-two let's do this
No longer afraid and useless
At least, that's what I tell myself

Fixation of the Self

I am in love with an idea
a figment of my imagination
there are no features to the face
no form to the silhouette
is it fact or fiction?
even I don't know the answer
it's a complex conundrum
to love someone you don't know
completely—without hesitation
these are the uncharted waters
in which I dive daily
sinking into the depths of what
can only be described as devotion
this is my discovery of self-love

The Kid Still Lives

I have to tell you a secret
the kid still lives
he hides in the depths of your heart
rummaging in the bowels of your brain
he surfaces as the twinkle in your eyes
and the sparkle of your soul
the kid still lives
perhaps you should set him free
perhaps, you should let him be

Crossroads

Meet me where the roads cross

There, you see life from the outside

But don't take too long

Before I move from my spot

The roads come together quick

A few seconds is all you've got

Meet me between a synapse and vein

Here, I find a merging of my brain and heart

But it doesn't always work

Because brains sometimes lose to love

Then act off of how you feel

And pray to the guide for signs from above

Meet me where I end and begin

Where, all roads come together

But mind where the roads cross

Be cautious not afraid

They make you who you are

And will continue to each decade

To the Boy I was and the Man I am

to the boy I was
I'm sorry
I let the world twist you
change you
they assaulted and
estranged you
I ask for forgiveness
I pray for your healing
I wish for your peace

                to the man I am
                  listen to your heart
                    let it be your guide
                      do not become
                        like the boy I once was
                  or like the revelation
                all will end
              in a flash of signs
          and destruction

IN MOURNING

Later

I saw you two days ago

We sat and talked

For hours we laughed

Some minutes we even cried

Tears flowed freely then dried

The sun sank and we watched the moon rise

At last we said our goodbyes

I said see you later

But later will never come now

The Griever's Insomnia

Every moment is a waking nightmare

there's no escape

no reprieve

I can't go to sleep

Because there, it haunts me

in my dreams

It's the ghost of memories past

The spirit of the present

and the casket where it resides

A wisp from the future

one where there's no you, just I

The moon starts up high

I watch time change

from old day unto new night

And hear the birds chirping

as moon and sun make their exchange

My warm blanket is

the tiniest veil of comfort

For the grief that surrounds me

the insomnia that drowns me

And the weight of my heavy lids

refusing to close

Tears on my Pillow

bodies are corked containers

we are vessels

energy is taken

placed

absorbed

and stored

like a glass full of water

ready to spill and overflow

we hold so much

anything

everything

until

we can't anymore

that's why my eyes are dry

my pillows are wet

and my slumber cries

from

tears on

my pillow

and a series of emotions

that I can no longer contain

Bittersweet

In this moment

I am a tear

A solemn display

A salty reminder

Faint is my echo

Forever is my memory

Today I may cry

Tomorrow I will smile

Bitter is the taste of leaving

Sweet is the time having spent together

Sepulchral

what is this feeling?
it unbuttons the heart
spilling tears on the floor
setting the very air alight
smearing hope against the skin
it is an ethereal present
a ghostly embrace

There Will Be

there will be tears
let them flow
cry yourself a river
a million times over

there will be longing
for the days of old
to travel back
before time unfolds

there will be memories
the greatest hits
a highlight reel
you can't forget

there will be comfort
in the hands that hold you
the shoulders that catch tears
and the people that surround you

there will be peace
surpassing all understanding
plugging the hollows in your heart
guiding you out the dark

there will be
all these things and more
as you navigate
the choppy waters of healing

To Ida

I felt you in the wind today
As I ran through the streets
I felt your gentle caress in the breeze
You carried my tears away

I see you in my mind always
As you embrace others in love
With divinity and soul lifting hugs
Blessing all who know your name

I felt you in my heart last night
When darkness enveloped me
And the tears first came
And you slipped away from the pain

I feel you in my soul tomorrow
Knowing you watch over me
Hoping that I make you proud
Waiting until we can hug again

Rise like Batter
(A tribute to Auntie) • *4/10/21*

The kitchen is a sacred place
It houses the spirits of my ancestors
They reign down from the heavens
Guiding us children in the ways of food

Whenever I enter the kitchen
I look up and ask for auntie
She guides me as I stir the pots
And holds my hands as I drop seasonings

We talk like the days before
My words echo against the walls
She tells me that she's proud of me
And holds me close as the tears fall

I watch the batter rise
As the oven's heat pulls it high
Waiting for the day
That I rise like batter and we reunite

save ur tears

oh daughter

oh son

save ur tears

don't u cry

like the sparrow

who has ur eye

I spread my wings

and now I fly

I know no sickness

I feel no pain

at long last

my crown I gain

worry not

my sweet child

live your life

and all the while

I watch over your every step

from beating heart

to final breath

IN EXPRESSION

Tides

I am the ocean

rolling across the beach

sweeping up sand

rushing in

rushing out

as tides

a reoccurring phenomenon

of the waves crashing

turning over

and over

tides

a continuous repetition

an unbreakable chain

water interwoven

and locked

like tides

I am an unstoppable force

Thunder

I want my voice to boom

Like thunder

Rolling across the hills

Commanding

Attention in every room

Silencing

Fears, doubts, and confusion

I want my voice to boom

Like thunder

Constant like movement

Echoing

In hearts and minds

Engraving

Memories for all time

I want my voice to boom

Like thunder

Red Light Special

Color theory says

That

The color red means passion

It also means love, anger, intensity

So

Why do we use it for red lights?

Are we supposed to

Stop

Our passions or love?

Are we not justified

In

Our anger and intensity?

I will not be stopped

Red

Lights, signs, tape

Cannot stop me

Flashing Yellow Lights

You must make a choice
When you come to flashing yellow lights
Either you will push
Full speed ahead
Or slowly you will stop, dead in your tracks

You have but a moment
Where you must make a split second decision
Either to hesitate
And kill your dreams
Or take the risk, and see what life brings

I've seen my share of reds
But it's the flashing yellow lights
That open doors
And unleash the flood
Lying in wait for that green light go

Green Light Go

Like the rose

Out the concrete

I

Grow

Like green light go

Simon never

Stopped me

I

Attract

Money and wealth

Accumulating sickening health

I

Seize

Every opportunity

Achieving my dreams

I

Grow

Like the rose

Out the concrete

On

My

Green

Light

Go

Canvas

Like clay to a potter

Or

Keyboards to a blogger

I

Yes I

Am molded and made

Like pencil on paper

Or

Acrylic on canvas

I

Yes I

Am created

And if necessary

Remade

Retrospection

the rejections are like little love letters

sending back unrequited love

and a directional arrow

in which the next target awaits,

arms wide and heart open,

for the gutting arrow of my words to find it.

the disappointments are a rush of feeling

pumping gallons of new blood into veins

that had seemingly withered and closed

succumbing to the numbness of reality,

forced open by the scratching of the heart,

allowing for the escape of my essence.

the insecurities are the whispers of characters

neither seen or born onto the page

as they wrestle with their brethren within my womb

clawing for an opportunity to take shape,

to embody emotion and personify my dreams,

like the oldest of memories being made real.

the impatience is a reminder notification

projecting all of the hours that were lost

where I poured my soul over others' work

instead of stretching my seconds into centuries,

ladling my conscience onto the page and canvas,

that others may marvel at the wonders I conjure.

the sleeplessness is a personification

capturing a most vivid likeness with delicate hands

painting the hurricane of my emotions

splattering it across my inner eyelids,

as it washes away the world around me,

and I am carried by the winds of obscurity into a creative stupor.

Steam & Showers

this is my sanctuary

and yet

it is also my coffin

steam rises

water falls

each droplet infused

with the spirit

of creativity

and the song of memory

washing wave

after wave

of emotions old and new

into the lather

of my soap

and rinsing

new stories to tell

into the depths

of my soul

I like my showers hot

with the windows steamed

I Write

I write sins
Not symphonies
Like a crypt keeper
I raise the dead

I write spells
Not scientific notation
I bend the universe to my will
Like a quadratic equation

I write in pictures
Not songs
I slay beasts and save realms
With the tools in my palms

I write with my truth
Not the lies of others
I do not stave off my work
Because of words from one's mother

art machine

you are a machine
a body with bones
made of gears
with a mind for
creating work
without ceasing or
rest

you are a machine
made for weaving the
old into new
and the intangible into
something that
is not only felt but is also
perceived and
heard

you are a machine
made from failed projects
and soiled dreams
running on the tears of
yesterday and
the hopes of tomorrow
you are
an incredible art machine
forevermore

the cult of creation

I know all too well
the cult of creation
I've knelt in their temple
and prayed to their god
I bathed in their sacred waters
born again, to start anew
I've preached their gospel
to both saints and sinners
I surrendered my tithes to
buy new crayons and paints
I've sat with the moon
crying into the dark
I beat and bruised my body
all for the sake of art
I know all too well
the cult of creation
and the lies they spread
with demons in your head
and a workstation as a bed

the artist trope

each morning opens with a series

of possibilities

until I leave the sanctuary of my studio

and open myself

to the attacks of the outside world

there are the stares

and the not so subtle whispers

that carry me

into conversations about masculinity

and sexuality

followed by the penetration of race by religion

all because

the stigma of the artist trope hangs over me

and I lean into it

more than I would really like to admit

but I don't kiss and tell

instead I let my work speak for itself

and mold myself

after my art and all the preconceived

notions that come with it

starving artist

this is a note to self

a memorandum

a contractual obligation

to remember

what it was like

being up all night

worrying about perceptions

of your work

and not your needs or your

fiscal responsibilities

choosing to starve both your

stomach and wallet

in pursuit of your dreams

or childish things

this is a letter to my alternative history

or parallel present

to cultivate your craft

and watch

the way you spend your

time and money

so that you are not the next great

household name

with a wave of fame and

two pennies

in your bank account to

show for it

To Be Continued

my soul has sailed

I am both the ocean and the boat it carries

the wind and the mast it blows through

the journey begins

as the horizon of land ends

like the roads that cross

I seek the isle of the lost

there's a man there

a boy really

whom I must claim

for now, the rest is unwritten

an ellipses or perhaps comma

putting the world on pause

PUBLICATIONS

Below is a list of poems from this collection that have been previously published, as well as the magazines and presses that stored them within one of their issues.

Afro Literary Magazine
"Rise Like Batter"

GutSlut Press
"70 minus 1"

Zero Readers Mag
"In the Darkness"

ACKNOWLEDGMENTS

First and foremost, thank you, God, for the patience and perseverance to complete this body of work. The road was a long and arduous one, as I opened myself up not only to the medium of poetry, but also to the various thoughts and feelings that I have explored whilst on this journey.

Secondly, thank you, Mom and Dad, for your continuous push for me to pursue my passions, no matter how outlandish they may seem and regardless of whatever strange place the journey may take me. You have always been the foundation for which the seeds of my labor were planted.

Thank you Gaga, for being my enthusiastic cheerleader. I know that you can't wait to brag to your friends about this as soon as you possibly can. Your sense of pride in me and my work pushes me to produce the very best work that I can. I hope that this, that I, make you proud.

Alex and Shawn, thank you for being my siblings. I'm not sure what else I could say that could possibly quantify the way that our bond empowers me and my artistry. I can only hope to be half as cool as you all. I hope that I, that this work, makes you all proud.

To the rest of my family and friends, thank you for your support. There were frenzied, unintelligible conversations about personification and existential dread that took shape in my work. There were early morning and late-night phone calls. There were moments of screaming into the void and losing sight of ourselves amid the process. Thank you for holding me up. Thank you hyping me up. I appreciate you.

Lastly, thank you, dear reader, for meeting me at the crossroads. I hope that if you, like me, are searching for yourself, that this work speaks to you. I pray that it keeps you company and comforts you on the journey. Take my hand and travel with me, as we forge ahead, and ultimately ride into the next chapter, regardless of where it is or what it looks like. Thank you for giving life to the work. I hope you enjoy. I hope you relate to it. I hope it speaks to you.

ABOUT ATMOSPHERE PRESS

Atmosphere Press is an independent, full-service publisher for excellent books in all genres and for all audiences. Learn more about what we do at atmospherepress.com.

We encourage you to check out some of Atmosphere's latest releases, which are available at Amazon.com and via order from your local bookstore:

Melody in Exile, by S.T. Grant

Covenant, by Kate Carter

Weightless, Woven Words, by Umar Siddiqui

Journeying: Flying, Family, Foraging, by Nicholas Ranson

Lexicon of the Body, by DM Wallace

Controlling Chaos, by Michael Estabrook

Almost a Memoir, by M.C. Rydel

Throwing the Bones, by Caitlin Jackson

Like Fire and Ice, by Eli

Sway, by Tricia Johnson

A Patient Hunger, by Skip Renker

The Carcass Undressed, by Linda Eguiliz

Poems That Wrote Me, by Karissa Whitson

Gnostic Triptych, by Elder Gideon

For the Moment, by Charnjit Gill

Battle Cry, by Jennifer Sara Widelitz

I woke up to words today, by Daniella Deutsch

Never Enough, by William Guest

Second Adolescence, by Joe Rolnicki

ABOUT THE AUTHOR

DRE HILL is an artist, storyteller, and apple juice enthusiast from Fort Worth, TX. He graduated from Drury University in 2021 with his B.A. in Animation and Writing, where he reignited his childhood passion for the written word. He has his many English professors to thank for that. He published his first two chapbooks, *i love you means nothing* through Alien Buddha Press and *Melanin: Black* through GutSlut Press in 2022. When not creating, Dre is often snuggling with his puppy, Jet, while watching Marvel movies. Find Dre at @drehillart on all platforms. His website is drehillart.com.